W9-BMR-235

MOST-USED WORDS AND PHRASES

Diamond Jubilee Series

John Robert Gregg

Louis A. Leslie

Charles E. Zoubek

Shorthand written by Charles Rader

GREGG

7 5

GREGG DIVISION

McGRAW-HILL BOOK COMPANY

New York   Chicago   Dallas   San Francisco
Toronto   London   Sydney

MOST-USED WORDS AND PHRASES, DIAMOND JUBILEE SERIES

Copyright © 1963 by McGraw-Hill Book Company, Inc. All Rights Reserved.
Copyright 1949 by McGraw-Hill Book Company, Inc. All Rights Reserved. This
book, or parts thereof, may not be reproduced in any form without permission of
the publishers.

7 8 9 10 11 12 WC WC 76 75 74 73 72 71 70

24592

Library of Congress Catalog Card No. 61-18133

Preface

Most-Used Words and Phrases, Diamond Jubilee Series, is a compilation of 3,822 words and 1,509 phrases classified according to the lessons of *Gregg Shorthand, Diamond Jubilee Series*. Each word and phrase, together with its shorthand outline, is listed according to the lesson and the principle of *Gregg Shorthand, Diamond Jubilee Series*, under which it can first be written.

Selection of Words

The words were taken from the first 10,000 words in order of frequency as indicated in the Horn-Peterson *Basic Vocabulary of Business Letters*, which contains 14,834 different words found in a count of 1,500,000 words of business letters chosen from 26 kinds of businesses. The words selected for inclusion in the lists of *Most-Used Words and Phrases* are those that are of the greatest usefulness to the stenographer in the business office.

Many of the first 10,000 words in order of frequency in the Horn-Peterson study are simple derivatives in *-ing*, *-s*, and *-ed*; and the student can easily form shorthand outlines for them from the primitive forms. Consequently, only a few of these simple derivatives have been included in *Most-Used Words and Phrases*. However, all derivatives that present some stenographic problems are given.

Selection of Phrases

The shorthand phrases in *Most-Used Words and Phrases* have been selected from a business-letter phrase-frequency count in which the authors analyzed the phrase content of 2,500 business letters containing more than 250,000 words. In this study the authors found 3,536 different phrases, 1,569 of which have been selected for inclusion in the lists of this book. Each phrase, with its shorthand outline, is listed in the lesson where it can first be written.

Distribution of Words and Phrases

As a result of the elimination of a number of word-building and phrasing principles, brief forms, and word beginnings and endings

iii

from the system, hundreds of additional useful business words and phrases can now be written in the early lessons of *Gregg Shorthand, Diamond Jubilee Series*. The availability of these additional words and phrases makes possible the construction of smooth, natural practice material almost from the first lesson.

Distribution of Words and Phrases

CHAPTER	WORDS	PHRASES
1	939	347
2	525	536
3	561	268
4	580	162
5	526	105
6	302	129
7	239	9
8	150	13
Totals	3,822	1,569

500 Most Frequently Used Business Words

A feature that teachers will find helpful is the list of the 500 most frequently used business words of the Horn-Peterson study presented in the order of their frequency. This list appears in the Appendix.

Index

At the back of *Most-Used Words and Phrases* is an alphabetical index of all words included in the book, together with an indication of the lesson in which they appear.

It is the hope of the authors that teachers will find the lists in *Most-Used Words and Phrases, Diamond Jubilee Series,* useful in their shorthand teaching.

LOUIS A. LESLIE
CHARLES E. ZOUBEK

Chapter
1

Lesson 1

▶ **S-Z, A, F, V**

face		safe		say	
phase		save		vase	

▶ **E**

easy		fees		see	
fee		sea		sees	

▶ **N**

knee		sane		seen	
navy		scene		vain	

▶ **M**

aim		may		mean	
main		me		same	

▶ **T**

ate		meat		stain	
east		neat		stay	
faced		safety		tea	
feet		seat		team	

▶ **D**

aid	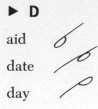	deed	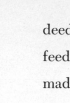	need	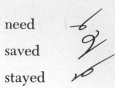
date		feed	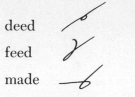	saved	
day		made		stayed	

Lesson 2

▶ **O**

foe	ℓ	phone	⌐	stove	
know		sew	ℓ	stow	
known		snow		toe	
no		so	ℓ	vote	
note		stone		zone	ℓ

▶ **R**

dear		near		store	
door		nor		storm	
drain		or		story	
drove		rate		tore	
fair		read		torn	
free		remain		trade	
freight		rename		treat	
more		road		wrote	

▶ **L**

deal		late		mail	
fail		lead		real	
feel		leave		relay	
floor		loan		retail	
lady		low		steal	

▶ **H**

hair		hear		hole	
haste		heat		home	
hate		heed		horn	
he		here		whole	

▶ **WORD ENDING** *-ing*

aiming		mailing		reading	
feeling		rating		trading	

▶ **ī**

die		life		my	
drive		light		night	
dry		line		rely	
dye		lining		right	
file		might		side	
height		mighty		sign	
hide		mile		style	
iron		mine		tire	

title   tried   write

▶ OMISSION OF MINOR VOWELS

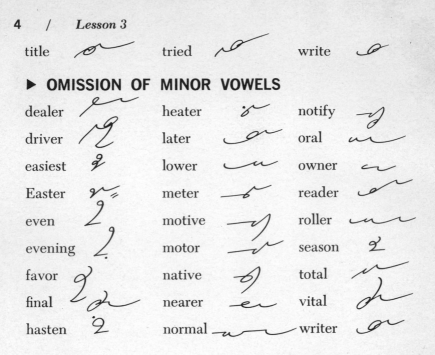

dealer	heater	notify
driver	later	oral
easiest	lower	owner
Easter	meter	reader
even	motive	roller
evening	motor	season
favor	native	total
final	nearer	vital
hasten	normal	writer

Lesson 3

▶ BRIEF FORMS

a	have	Mr.
am	hour	not
an	I	our
are	in	well
at	it	will

▶ PHRASES

Have

have made   have not   he may have

he will have	I have tried	may have
I have	I may have	might have
I have made	I will have	will have
I have not	it will have	will not have

I

I am	I mean	I say
I drove	I might	I see
I fear	I need	I will
I feel	I need not	I will not
I know	I remain	I wrote

Will, Well

| he will | so well | will not |
| he will not | well known | will write |

Miscellaneous

| in it | it will | may not |
| in our | it will not | might not |

▶ LEFT S-Z

dates	frames	knows
days	frozen	ladies
fails	highest	lease
favors	homes	leasing
feels	hours	least
files	its	lines

means		readers		series	
most		realize		sides	
names		release		slight	
needs		rights		source	
niece		rise		styles	
notes		rose		wholesale	
ours		sales		wills	
raise		seats		writers	
rates		seems		zeal	

► **P**

deep		plain		proposed	
hope		plate		provide	
open		please		ropes	
paid		pleased		soap	
pair		pleasing		space	
paper		pole		spare	
pay		post		speed	
payroll		premium		supplied	
pays		prepare		suppose	
people		private		supposed	
piece		proceed		supreme	
pipes		promote		type	
place		propose		typewriter	

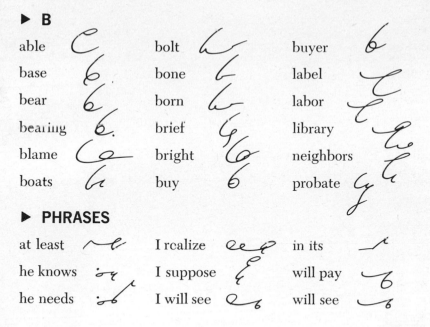

▶ B

able	bolt	buyer
base	bone	label
bear	born	labor
bearing	brief	library
blame	bright	neighbors
boats	buy	probate

▶ PHRASES

at least	I realize	in its
he knows	I suppose	will pay
he needs	I will see	will see

Lesson 4

▶ SH

shade	share	sheets
shades	shares	show
shape	she	shown
shaped	sheep	shows

▶ CH

chain	cheap	chief
chains	cheaper	chose
chair	cheese	chosen

each	reach	reaches
porch	reached	torch

▶ **J**

age	changed	pages
agencies	changes	rage
agency	oblige	range
aging	obliged	siege
change	page	storage

▶ **PHRASES**

each day	each night	he reaches

▶ **OO**

blue	July	prove
boots	June	proved
choose	juries	proven
do	jury	prune
drew	juvenile	remove
fireproof	loose	roof
food	lose	room
fruit	move	root
hereto	noon	route
jewel	pool	routine
jewelers	poor	rule
jewelry	proof	shoe

shoes	too	two
spoon	tool	who
sure	tour	whom
to	true	whose

▶ K

acre	corn	make
bouquet	corner	makes
break	coupon	making
broke	course	reclaim
cake	courtesy	recline
came	cream	remake
care	cried	retake
case	crude	sake
cave	cry	scheme
claim	decay	school
claims	declare	score
clean	decline	screw
clear	decrease	smoke
clearer	keep	specific
close	keys	spoke
coal	lake	take
coast	like	taken
cool	locate	vacancies

▶ G *(Gay)*

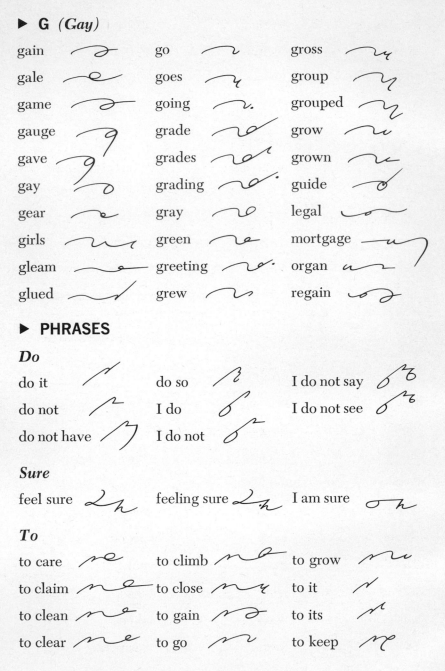

gain	go	gross
gale	goes	group
game	going	grouped
gauge	grade	grow
gave	grades	grown
gay	grading	guide
gear	gray	legal
girls	green	mortgage
gleam	greeting	organ
glued	grew	regain

▶ PHRASES

Do

do it	do so	I do not say
do not	I do	I do not see
do not have	I do not	

Sure

feel sure	feeling sure	I am sure

To

to care	to climb	to grow
to claim	to close	to it
to clean	to gain	to its
to clear	to go	to keep

to take 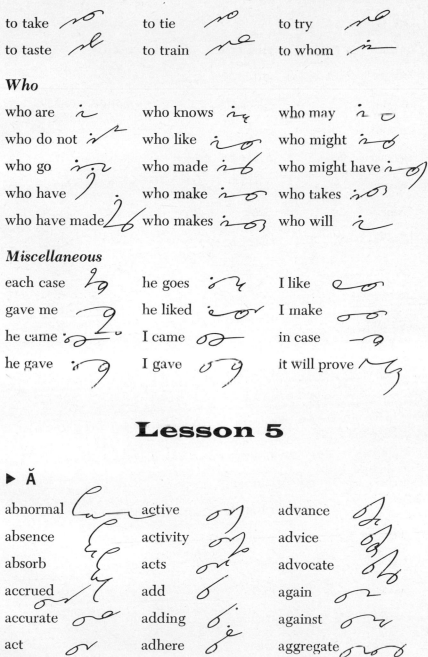   to tie   to try

to taste   to train   to whom

Who

who are   who knows   who may

who do not   who like   who might

who go   who made   who might have

who have   who make   who takes

who have made   who makes   who will

Miscellaneous

each case   he goes   I like

gave me   he liked   I make

he came   I came   in case

he gave   I gave   it will prove

Lesson 5

▶ Ă

abnormal   active   advance

absence   activity   advice

absorb   acts   advocate

accrued   add   again

accurate   adding   against

act   adhere   aggregate

ago	astray	casting
agree	attached	catch
alone	attractive	chairman
ample	average	chance
amplify	back	class
apiece	backed	classified
appeal	backs	cordial
appear	bad	cracked
applies	bag	data
apply	baggage	draft
approach	bags	drag
approached	balance	fabric
approval	barrel	fact
approve	battery	factory
approved	black	facts
arrange	branch	fast
arrive	branches	flag
arrives	campaign	flat
as	capacity	gas
aside	capital	gasoline
ask	carry	glance
assurance	cash	glass
assure	cashier	graphs
assures	cast	gratified

gratifying	map	ratify
habit	maps	sacrifice
had	master	sad
half	match	salary
happen	matches	salesman
happens	material	sample
happy	matters	sash
has	narrower	scrap
hats	package	sedan
jam	paragraph	staff
lack	pass	stamp
lamps	passed	tags
last	past	task
lasting	plan	track
lasts	plans	tract
machine	proposal	tractor
machines	rag	traffic
magazine	ran	traveler
man	rapid	vast

▶ Ä

alarm	army	car
arm	art	cargo
arms	bargain	carload

charge		farms		marked	
charged		harm		marks	
charges		jar		park	
charming		large		sharp	
dark		March		star	
far		margin		start	
farm		mark		starts	

▶ **Ĕ**

accept		check		errors	
address		checked		establishing	
addressed		checks		etc.	
any		chest		federal	
assets		closest		fell	
basket		currency		fellow	
bed		desk		fellows	
beg		edges		finest	
belt		effect		fresh	
best		effective		get	
better		elect		getting	
bread		else		guess	
cabinet		enable		harvest	
cancel		enamel		head	
cheapest		error		heads	

heartless	medal	select
heavy	medicine	seller
help	messages	sells
helped	met	semester
helpless	metal	sense
helplessness	nearest	separate
helps	needless	set
hopeless	negative	settle
hotel	net	shell
jelly	parcel	shelves
kept	pleasure	sketch
largest	pledge	slightest
latest	presence	slowest
led	pressure	specified
left	professor	specify
leg	protect	spread
less	protest	step
lessons	ready	supremacy
let	regret	telegraph
letter	relative	telephone
letters	remedy	tell
lowest	rest	test
market	said	testify
measure	secretary	tests

treasure	treasury	verify
treasurer	verified	wrenches

▶ ĭ

admit	dictate	hit
April	did	if
arisen	dig	ignore
artist	dishes	illness
been	drastic	imagine
benefit	drill	inactive
bid	elastic	kill
bidding	facilitate	kitchen
bids	familiar	liberal
billing	fill	liberty
bills	finance	list
bridge	finish	listen
bridges	fiscal	little
built	fit	live
busy	gift	lives
chemistry	give	merit
chickens	given	middle
Christmas	gives	milk
cigars	guilty	mill
city	him	miss
clipping	hinges	notice

omit	principal	since
original	prohibit	sincere
pencil	remit	solicit
pick	rid	spirit
pig	risk	statistics
pigs	river	still
pin	ship	territory
pins	shipped	tickets
practice	shipper	tip
predict	sickness	trip
prettiest	similar	vicinity
pretty	simple	visit

▶ OBSCURE VOWEL

answer	first	major
certificate	fur	prefer
certified	grocery	search
certify	her	serve
church	hosiery	service
circle	hurry	surprise
clerk	hurt	surprised
earn	journal	teacher
earnest	larger	teachers
firm	learn	tracer
firms	ledger	urge

▶ OVER *Th*

bath		smooth		thick	
blacksmith		teeth		thicker	
booth		theater		thickness	
death		theme		thin	
faith		then		thinner	
method		these		tooth	

▶ UNDER *Th*

birth		health		thread	
birthday		healthy		three	
both		lathe		throat	
clothing		north		through	
earth		thorough		throw	
growth		though		thrown	

▶ PHRASES

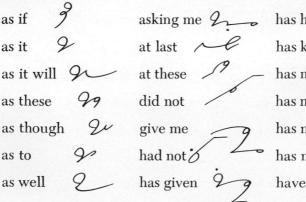

as if		asking me		has had	
as it		at last		has known	
as it will		at these		has made	
as these		did not		has met	
as though		give me		has no	
as to		had not		has not	
as well		has given		have given	

have had	I have had	since then
he did	I left	so large
he did not	I live	these are
he fell	I met	through its
he felt	I notice	through these
he gets	I ran	to cancel
he left	I read	to carry
he lives	I said	to cash
he said	if it	to catch
I did	if my	to get
I did not	if so	to give
I felt	if these	to tell
I get	in fact	to these
I give	in these	to travel
I guess	it has	who have had

▶ BRIEF FORMS

but	is	with
can	Mrs.	withdrew
cannot	of	you
can't	that	your
his	the	yours

▶ PHRASES

Can

can have	he can	he can make

he can't	I cannot	who can
I can	I can see	who cannot

Is, His

as it is	if it is	it is
he is	in his	she is
he is not	is it	she is not
he is the	is not	to his
here is	is the	who is

Of

of his	of its	of the
of it	of our	of these

That

as that	is that	that have
as to that	is that the	that is
ask that	of that	that is not
at that	realize that	that is the
hope that	so that	that it
hope that the	so that the	that it has
hoping that	that are	that it is
if that is	that are not	that it will
in that	that do not	that its

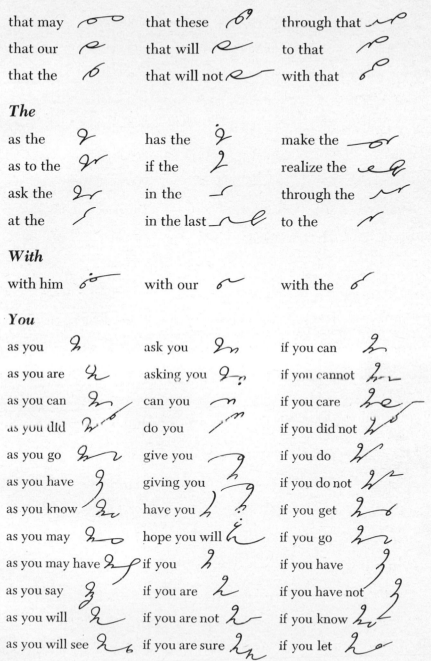

that may

that our

that the

that these

that will

that will not

through that

to that

with that

The

as the

as to the

ask the

at the

has the

if the

in the

in the last

make the

realize the

through the

to the

With

with him

with our

with the

You

as you

as you are

as you can

as you did

as you go

as you have

as you know

as you may

as you may have

as you say

as you will

as you will see

ask you

asking you

can you

do you

give you

giving you

have you

hope you will

if you

if you are

if you are not

if you are sure

if you can

if you cannot

if you care

if you did not

if you do

if you do not

if you get

if you go

if you have

if you have not

if you know

if you let

if you need	you cannot	you may
if you see	you cannot see	you may have
if you will	you can't	you may not
if you will have	you did	you might
if you will see	you did not	you might have
of you	you do	you might not
reach you	you do not	you need
serving you	you have	you need not
to you	you have had	you say
with you	you have made	you see
you are	you have not	you will
you are not	you have seen	you will have
you can	you know	you will not
you can have	you made	you will not have
you can see	you make	you will see

Your

as to your	if your	with your
as your	of your	your letter
ask your	of yours	your name
have your	to your	your needs

Chapter

2

Lesson 7

▶ ŏ

adopt	copper	golf
anybody	correct	got
block	cost	hog
blotter	costing	holiday
body	costs	honest
borrow	cottage	honesty
borrowers	crop	honor
bronze	cross	hop
catalogue	crossed	hospital
clock	dock	hot
collar	doctor	job
collect	dog	jobber
college	dollar	knowledge
co-operate	drop	lobby
co-operative	follow	lock
copies	foreign	logs

23

loss	often	promised
lost	oftener	proper
lot	on	property
mob	operate	prospect
model	opposed	prospective
moderate	opposite	remodeling
modify	orange	rob
mop	origin	rock
moral	pocket	rod
nobody	policy	shop
observe	polish	soft
occur	politics	solid
occurrence	popular	solve
off	positive	sorrow
offer	problem	spot
office	profit	stock
officers	project	stop
offset	promise	top

▶ **AW**

abroad	ball	broader
all	baseball	brought
author	bought	call
authoritative	broad	caught
auto	broadcasting	cause

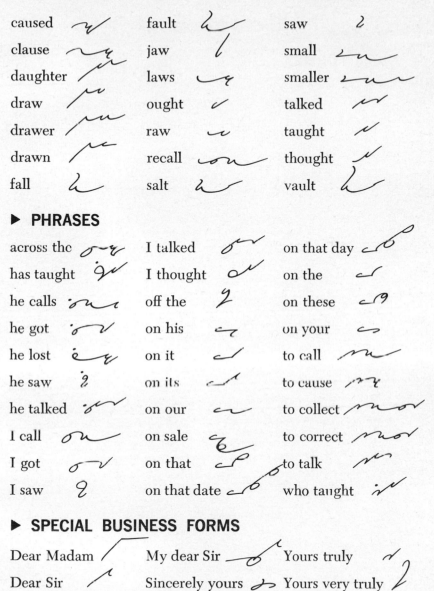

caused	fault	saw
clause	jaw	small
daughter	laws	smaller
draw	ought	talked
drawer	raw	taught
drawn	recall	thought
fall	salt	vault

▶ PHRASES

across the	I talked	on that day
has taught	I thought	on the
he calls	off the	on these
he got	on his	on your
he lost	on it	to call
he saw	on its	to cause
he talked	on our	to collect
I call	on sale	to correct
I got	on that	to talk
I saw	on that date	who taught

▶ SPECIAL BUSINESS FORMS

Dear Madam	My dear Sir	Yours truly
Dear Sir	Sincerely yours	Yours very truly

Lesson 8

▶ BRIEF FORMS

be		goods		therefore	
before		put		therein	
being		shall		thereon	
by		their		this	
for		there		which	
good		thereby		would	

▶ PHRASES

Be

be sure		if it will be		that will be	
being sure		if you can be		who can be	
can be		if you will be		who may be	
can be sure		it will be		who might be	
cannot be		it will not be		who will be	
can't be		may be		will be	
he can be		may not be		will not be	
he will be		might be		would be	
he would be		might not be		would not be	
I can be		need be		you can be	
I cannot be		need not be		you may be	
I can't be		she may be		you may be sure	
I will be		that it will be		you will be	
I would be		that may be		you will not be	

By

by it	by that	by which
by its	by the	by you
by mail	by these	by your

For

for his	for that	for whom
for it	for the	for you
for its	for the last	for your
for me	for the past	for your letter
for Mr.	for their	before that
for most	for these	before the
for my	for which	before you
for our	for which the	before your

Good

as good	good deal

Shall

I shall	I shall make	shall not
I shall be	I shall not	shall not be
I shall have	I shall see	you shall have

There, their

as there	if there is	of their
as there is	if there will	that their
if there are	is there	that there are

that there is	there may	there will be
there are	there may be	there would be
there is	there will	to their

This

as this	in this case	this is the
at this	in this matter	this letter
before this	of this	this man
by this	on this	this matter
do this	on this matter	this may
for this	since this	this may be
hope that this	that this	this means
if this	that this is	this will
if this is	this can be	this would
if this is not	this date	this would be
if this is the	this is	to this
in this	this is not	with this

Which

in which	on which the	which means
in which the	which is	which you
in which you	which is the	which you can
of which	which may	which you may
on which	which may be	with which

Would

as you would	he would	I would
as you would be	he would have	I would have

I would not	that would be	would have
if you would	who would	you would
if you would be	who would be	you would be
if you would have	who would have	you would have
that would	who would not	you would not

▶ WORD ENDING -ly

actively	finally	nicely
amply	firmly	normally
badly	freely	only
barely	highly	originally
briefly	honestly	positively
clearly	inevitably	possibly
closely	largely	principally
cordially	lately	properly
correctly	legally	rapidly
costly	likely	rarely
daily	locally	separately
deeply	mainly	simply
earlier	manly	sincerely
earliest	materially	slightly
early	merely	strictly
earnestly	mostly	surely
fairly	namely	thoroughly
favorably	nearly	totally

Lesson 9

▶ WORD ENDING -tion

action	mission	profession
allocation	motion	professional
application	national	promotion
authorization	nationally	proportion
cancellation	obligation	proportionate
caution	occasion	proposition
collection	occasionally	propositions
collision	operation	protection
co-operation	option	provision
corporation	physician	ration
correction	portion	relation
declaration	position	section
election	possession	sectional
eradication	precaution	selection
fashion	preparation	session
irrigation	prescription	supposition
location	prevention	vacation

▶ WORD ENDINGS -cient, -ciency

ancient	efficient	proficiency
efficiency	patient	proficient

▶ WORD ENDING -tial

beneficial	especially	essential

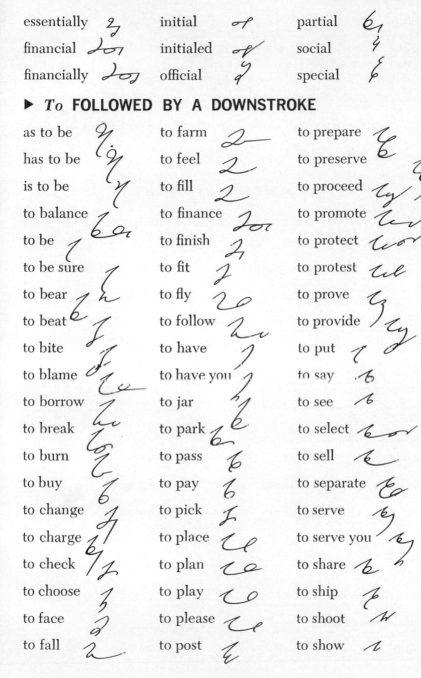

essentially		initial		partial	
financial		initialed		social	
financially		official		special	

▶ *To* FOLLOWED BY A DOWNSTROKE

as to be		to farm		to prepare	
has to be		to feel		to preserve	
is to be		to fill		to proceed	
to balance		to finance		to promote	
to be		to finish		to protect	
to be sure		to fit		to protest	
to bear		to fly		to prove	
to beat		to follow		to provide	
to bite		to have		to put	
to blame		to have you		to say	
to borrow		to jar		to see	
to break		to park		to select	
to burn		to pass		to sell	
to buy		to pay		to separate	
to change		to pick		to serve	
to charge		to place		to serve you	
to check		to plan		to share	
to choose		to play		to ship	
to face		to please		to shoot	
to fall		to post		to show	

to slide	to supply	to visit
to spare	to suppose	to which
to specify	to surprise	to which the
to speed	to survey	to which you
to spread	to verify	to which you are

Lesson 10

▶ **ND**

assigned	end	lend
band	fastened	lined
bind	find	loaned
binder	friend	mind
bindery	gained	opened
bond	grand	owned
bonded	grind	pending
brand	happened	phoned
burned	island	planned
calendar	kind	remainder
candy	kindest	remained
canned	kindness	remind
cleaned	land	reminded
cylinder	lands	render
earned	learned	sand

| signed | | splendid | | trained | |
| spend | | surrender | | trend | |

▶ NT

absent		current		plenty	
agent		event		prevent	
agents		genteel		prevented	
apparent		gentle		printer	
applicant		grant		rent	
aunt		granted		rental	
bent		guarantee		rented	
carpenter		hints		sent	
cent		paint		silent	
center		parents		spent	
central		plant		talent	
centralized		planted		urgent	
cogent		pleasant		vacant	

Ant-, End-, Ent-

anticipate		entire		indications	
anticipation		entirely		intact	
antique		entry		intelligence	
endorse		indicate		intelligent	
endorsed		indicates		intelligently	
endorser		indication		into	

▶ PHRASES

aren't		I learned		to plant	
as you will find		I sent		to prevent	
didn't		if you didn't		to print	
don't		if you don't		to spend	
hadn't		into it		who didn't	
hasn't		into that		who isn't	
haven't		into the		will find	
he didn't		into these		wouldn't	
he finds		into this		you aren't	
he isn't		isn't		you didn't	
I didn't		isn't it		you don't	
I don't		to bind		you haven't	
I find		to find		you will find	
I haven't		to paint		you wouldn't	

▶ SES

access		auspices		chances	
addresses		balances		classes	
advances		bases		clauses	
advices		basis		closes	
analysis		braces		courses	
arises		cases		criticism	
assessed		causes		faces	
assist		census		finances	

glasses		nurses		proposes	
horses		offices		releases	
leases		passes		says	
lenses		places		services	
losses		premises		sister	
mattresses		presses		sizes	
necessary		prices		sources	
necessitate		process		spaces	
necessity		processes		suspend	
notices		promises		versus	

Lesson 11

▶ BRIEF FORMS

and		hands		them	
could		handle		they	
from		send		was	
hand		should		when	

▶ PHRASES

And

and are		and our		and the	
and have		and say		and their	
and his		and see		and they	
and is		and that		and was	
and let		and that is		and which	

and will ⟋ and will be ⟋ and will not ⟋

Could

could be ⟋ I could ⟋ who could ⟋
could not ⟋ I could be ⟋ you could ⟋
could not be ⟋ I could not ⟋ you could be ⟋
he could ⟋ I could see ⟋ you could have ⟋
he could not ⟋ I couldn't ⟋ you could not ⟋
he couldn't ⟋ if you could ⟋ you could see ⟋

From

from him ⟋ from that ⟋ from this ⟋
from his ⟋ from the ⟋ from you ⟋
from it ⟋ from them ⟋ from which ⟋
from our ⟋ from these ⟋ hear from you ⟋

Send

send him ⟋ send this ⟋ sending the ⟋
send them ⟋ send you ⟋ sending you ⟋

Should

he should ⟋ I should like ⟋ who should ⟋
he should be ⟋ I should say ⟋ who should be ⟋
he should have ⟋ should be ⟋ you should ⟋
I should ⟋ should have ⟋ you should be ⟋
I should be ⟋ should not be ⟋ you should have ⟋
I should have ⟋ shouldn't ⟋ you should not ⟋

Them

ask them 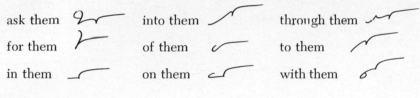   into them   through them

for them   of them   to them

in them   on them   with them

They

as they	they are	they don't
as they are	they are not	they have
before they	they can	they may
if they	they can be	they may be
if they are	they can have	they will
if they are not	they cannot	they will be
if they can	they can't	they will have
if they would	they could	they will not
if they would be	they could not	they will see
that they	they did	they would
that they are	they do	they would not
that they will	they do not	they would not be

Was

he was	it wasn't	this was the
he wasn't	that it was	was it
I was	that there was	was that
it was	there was	was the
it was the	this was	which was

When

when our		when the		when they	
when that		when these		when this	

▶ RD

accordance		guard		pardoned	
answered		hard		preferred	
appeared		harder		prepared	
assured		hardly		record	
bird		hazard		rendered	
board		heard		retired	
border		hired		seaboard	
burden		ignored		stored	
card		occurred		surrendered	
cord		offered		third	
favored		orchard		tired	
garden		pardon		toward	

▶ LD

billed		children		filed	
build		cold		filled	
builders		drilled		fold	
called		entitled		folded	
canceled		failed		folder	
child		field		gold	

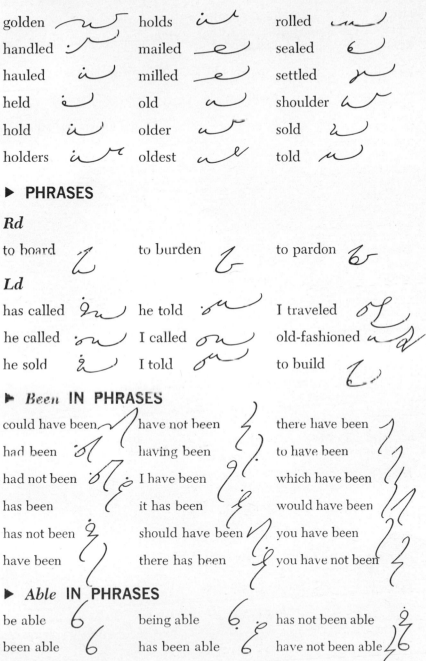

golden	holds	rolled
handled	mailed	sealed
hauled	milled	settled
held	old	shoulder
hold	older	sold
holders	oldest	told

▶ PHRASES

Rd

to board   to burden   to pardon

Ld

has called   he told   I traveled

he called   I called   old-fashioned

he sold   I told   to build

▶ *Been* IN PHRASES

could have been   have not been   there have been

had been   having been   to have been

had not been   I have been   which have been

has been   it has been   would have been

has not been   should have been   you have been

have been   there has been   you have not been

▶ *Able* IN PHRASES

be able   being able   has not been able

been able   has been able   have not been able

he may be able

he should be able

he will be able

he will not be able

he would be able

I have not been able

I shall be able

I shall not be able

I will be able

to be able

will be able

you may be able

you should be able

you will be able

you would be able

Chapter
3

Lesson 13

▶ **BRIEF FORMS**

enclose		orders		were	
enclosed		soon		work	
enclosure		sooner		worked	
glad		thank		worker	
gladly		thanked		year	
order		thanks		years	
ordered		very		yesterday	

▶ **PHRASES**

Enclose

he enclosed   I enclose   you enclosed

Glad

be glad   I am glad   shall be glad

he will be glad   I shall be glad   they will be glad

he would be glad   I should be glad   will be glad

Order

in order   in order that   in order that the

41

Thank

thank you	thank you for the	thank you for your
thank you for	thank you for this	to thank you for

Very

very glad	very good	very well

Were

if it were	there were	were not

▶ U

above	colored	famous
adjust	couple	hunting
adjusts	cover	illustrate
ambitious	covered	illustration
annum	covers	illustrations
apparatus	cup	industry
blood	cups	just
bonus	cut	justice
bud	does	justified
bulbs	drug	justify
bulk	duck	justly
bus	dug	luck
butter	dust	mud
chorus	enormous	muslin
color	enough	nervous

none	reduction	sufficient
number	religious	thus
numbered	rough	tough
nut	rub	truck
oven	rubber	trust
plug	shovels	unable
plus	status	uneven
product	stuff	up
production	suction	upper
productive	suffer	us
prosperous	suffered	utterly

▶ ŎŌ

book	foot	pull
looked	full	pulled
bookkeeping	fully	push
booklet	hook	stood
bushel	look	sugar
cook	looked	took

▶ **PHRASES**

Does

does not	he does	this does not
does not have	he does not	who doesn't
doesn't	that does not	which does

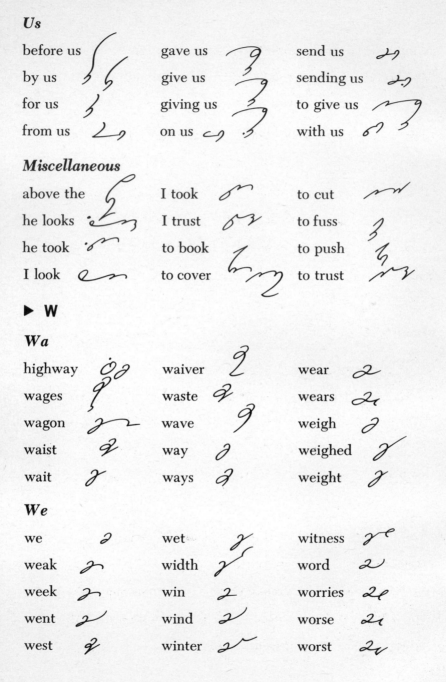

Us

before us	gave us	send us
by us	give us	sending us
for us	giving us	to give us
from us	on us	with us

Miscellaneous

above the	I took	to cut
he looks	I trust	to fuss
he took	to book	to push
I look	to cover	to trust

▶ **W**

Wa

highway	waiver	wear
wages	waste	wears
wagon	wave	weigh
waist	way	weighed
wait	ways	weight

We

we	wet	witness
weak	width	word
week	win	worries
went	wind	worse
west	winter	worst

Wi

wide		wire		wise	
wife		wired		wives	

Wo

walk		war		water	
wall		warm		woe	
walnut		warrant		won't	
want		wash		worn	
wanted		watch		woven	

Woo

wonder		wood		wool	
wondering		woods		woolen	

▶ SW

swam		sweet		swivel	
swear		swell		swollen	
sweater		switch		sworn	

▶ PHRASES

We

as we		if we can be		if we have	
as we are		if we cannot		we are	
as we have		if we could		we are not	
if we		if we do		we are sure	
if we can		if we don't		we call	

we can	we feel sure	we mean
we can be	we filled	we might
we can have	we find	we might be able
we can make	we get	we need
we can say	we give	we note
we cannot	we got	we notice
we cannot be	we have	we shall
we can't	we have been	we shall be
we could	we have been able	we shall be able
we could be	we have given	we shall be glad
we could have	we have had	we shall have
we could not	we have made	we shall mail
we couldn't	we have not	we shall make
we did	we have not been	we shall need
we did not	we have not been able	we shall not
we didn't	we have not had	we shall not be able
we do	we know	we shall see
we do not	we made	we should
we do not say	we mailed	we should be
we do not see	we make	we should have
we don't	we may	we should like
we enclose	we may be	we should not like
we failed	we may be able	we should say
we feel	we may have	we shouldn't

we take	we will	we would be glad
we thank you for	we will be	we would have
we thank you for the	we will have	we would like
we thank you for your	we will not	we would not
we took	we will not be	we would not be able
we tried	we will see	we wouldn't
we trust	we would	which we
we try	we would be	which we are

Lesson 14

▶ WH

| whale | wheel | whip |
| wheat | while | white |

▶ THE SOUND OF W IN THE BODY OF A WORD

acquainted	likewise	quota
adequate	liquid	quote
always	queen	railway
Broadway	query	requisition
dwelling	quick	roadway
equip	quicker	square
equipped	quickest	squarely
hardware	quit	twice
inadequate	quite	twin

▶ **TED**

accepted	hesitated	protested
acted	homestead	quoted
adapted	illustrated	rated
adjusted	indicated	related
admitted	lifted	remitted
adopted	limited	rested
affected	liquidated	routed
anticipated	listed	selected
asserted	located	separated
attested	marketed	solicited
benefited	neglected	started
coasted	noted	steady
collected	omitted	tested
co-operated	operated	treated
corrected	pasted	visited
dated	posted	waited
fitted	protected	wasted

Others

studied	study	today

▶ **DED**

added	deduct	deduction
dead	deducted	deductions

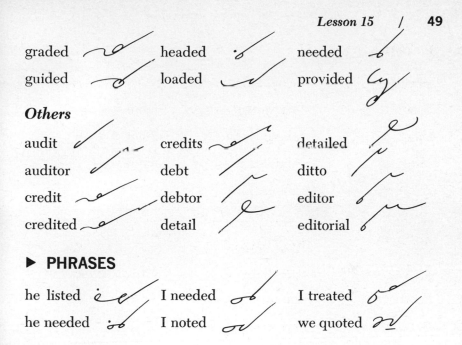

graded	headed	needed
guided	loaded	provided

Others

audit	credits	detailed
auditor	debt	ditto
credit	debtor	editor
credited	detail	editorial

▶ PHRASES

he listed	I needed	I treated
he needed	I noted	we quoted

Lesson 15

▶ BRIEF FORMS

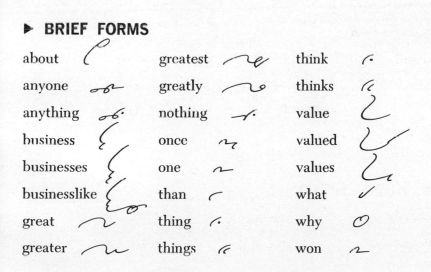

about	greatest	think
anyone	greatly	thinks
anything	nothing	value
business	once	valued
businesses	one	values
businesslike	than	what
great	thing	why
greater	things	won

▶ PHRASES

About

about it	about the	about which
about its	about them	about you
about my	about these	about your
about that	about this	

One

any one	one thing	one year
each one	one-half	only one
for one	one way	this one

Than

less than	less than the than the

Thing, Think

as you think	if they think	to think
do you think	if you think	we do not think
I do not think	same thing	who think
I think	they think	you think

What

what are	what is	what will
what has been	what is the	what will be

▶ WORD ENDING *-ble*

acceptable	adjustable	agreeable
adaptable	advisable	applicable

appreciable  eligible possible

available equitable profitable

cable favorable reliable

capable feasible salable

double liable table

doubled payable trouble

▶ WORD BEGINNING *Re-*

reappear refers resale

reason refining research

reasonable reflect reservation

reasonably reflected reserve

reasons region reserved

rebate register reservoir

receipt registered resist

receive rejected resources

recent repair respect

reception repaired respectively

rechecked repeat respondent

reciprocate repeated response

refer repeatedly reveal

reference replace reverse

referred replied revise

referring reproduction revision

Lesson 16

▶ OI

annoyance	coin	oil
annoyed	corduroy	point
appointed	hoist	poison
avoid	join	royal
boiled	joined	soil
boiler	joint	soiled
boy	jointly	spoiled
boys	joy	toy
choice	loyal	voice
coil	noise	void

▶ PHRASES

to boil	to join	to point

▶ MAN

manage	managers	romance
manager	manner	woman

▶ MEN

amend	immensely	mental
amended	many	mentally
cement	meant	mention
freshmen	men	mentioned

salesmen  tremendous women

▶ **MIN**

administer mineral prominence

aluminum minute prominent

eliminate nominal prominently

▶ **MON**

harmonize lemon month

harmony money monthly

▶ **MEM, MUM**

member memorial minimum

memo memory remember

▶ **PHRASES**

as many I mention these men

each month I mentioned this month

few minutes in this manner to mention

few months in this month's we mention

he mentioned so many you mentioned

▶ **WORD BEGINNING** *Be-*

became begins believer

because behalf below

began behind besides

begin belief betray

beginning believe beyond

Lesson 17

▶ **BRIEF FORMS**

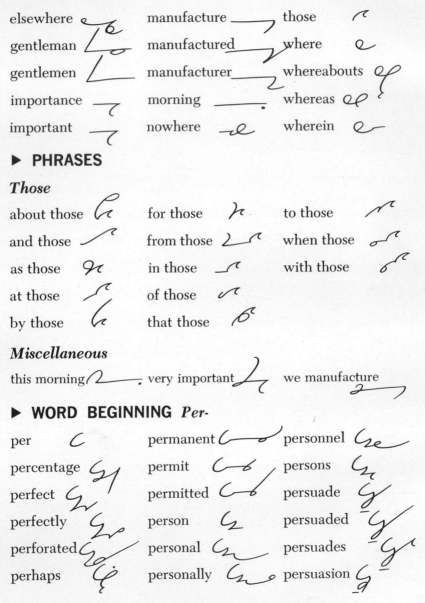

elsewhere	manufacture	those
gentleman	manufactured	where
gentlemen	manufacturer	whereabouts
importance	morning	whereas
important	nowhere	wherein

▶ **PHRASES**

Those

about those	for those	to those
and those	from those	when those
as those	in those	with those
at those	of those	
by those	that those	

Miscellaneous

this morning   very important   we manufacture

▶ **WORD BEGINNING** *Per-*

per	permanent	personnel
percentage	permit	persons
perfect	permitted	persuade
perfectly	person	persuaded
perforated	personal	persuades
perhaps	personally	persuasion

▶ **WORD BEGINNING** *Pur-*

purchase

purchased

purchases

purchasing

purloin

purple

▶ **PHRASES**

per cent

per hour

per month

to permit

to persuade

to purchase

▶ **WORD BEGINNING** *De-*

debit

decide

decided

decidedly

decision

delay

delayed

delays

deliberate

delighted

deliver

delivered

deliveries

depend

dependable

depended

dependent

depends

depleted

deposit

deposited

depositor

depository

deposits

depot

derive

deserve

design

designed

designer

designs

desirable

desire

desired

desires

desirous

▶ **WORD BEGINNING** *Dĭ*

diligently

direct

directed

direction

directly

director

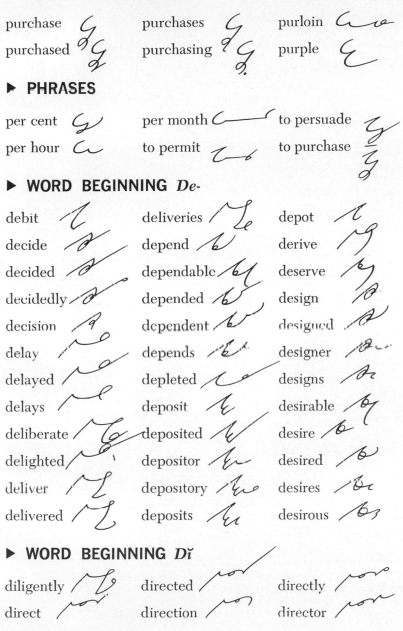

▶ PHRASES

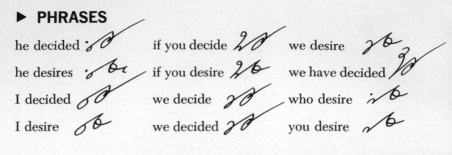

he decided   if you decide   we desire

he desires   if you desire   we have decided

I decided   we decide   who desire

I desire   we decided   you desire

Chapter

4

Lesson 19

▶ **BRIEF FORMS**

accompanied	hereafter	present
advertise	immediate	presented
after	immediately	represent
aftermath	must	representative
afternoon	opportunity	represented
afterthought	part	represents
companies	participate	wish
company	parties	wished
departing	party	wishes

▶ **PHRASES**

After

after that	after them	after this
after the	after these	after which

Must

he must	he must be	he must have

57

I must	she must	who must
I must be	she must be	who must be
I must have	that must be	you must
I must say	they must	you must be
must be	we must	you must be able
must have	we must have	you must have

Miscellaneous

at present	if you wish	to part
I wish	on our part	to present

▶ Ū

accusation	human	tube
accuse	peculiar	unique
acute	prosecute	unit
argue	prosecution	unite
beautify	pure	united
bureau	refusal	unusually
cubic	refused	usual
cure	refuses	utilization
few	review	view
fewer	reviews	viewed
fuel	tribune	views

▶ PHRASES

few days	in view	to prosecute
I refuse	to beautify	

▶ WORD ENDING *-ment*

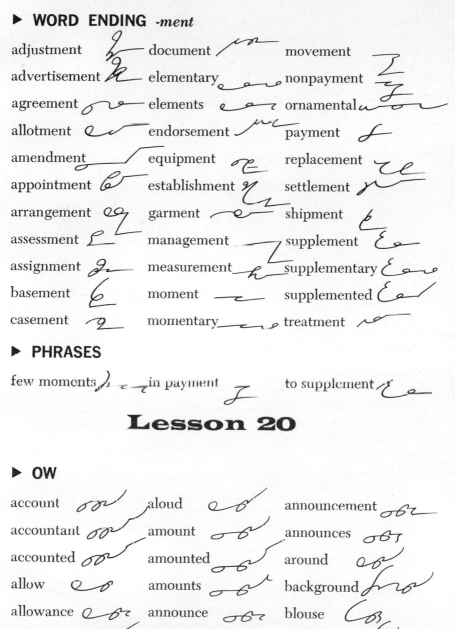

adjustment	document	movement
advertisement	elementary	nonpayment
agreement	elements	ornamental
allotment	endorsement	payment
amendment	equipment	replacement
appointment	establishment	settlement
arrangement	garment	shipment
assessment	management	supplement
assignment	measurement	supplementary
basement	moment	supplemented
casement	momentary	treatment

▶ PHRASES

few moments   in payment   to supplement

Lesson 20

▶ OW

account	aloud	announcement
accountant	amount	announces
accounted	amounted	around
allow	amounts	background
allowance	announce	blouse
allowed	announced	bound

brown		flowers		pound	
clown		found		pounds	
council		founded		powder	
counsel		foundry		power	
count		ground		proud	
counted		house		round	
counter		household		sound	
county		houses		south	
cow		loud		southeast	
crowd		mount		surround	
doubt		mounted		towels	
doubted		mouth		tower	
doubtless		now		town	
down		ounce		voucher	
flour		plow		warehouse	

▶ PHRASES

he found		I found		we count	
I doubt		in our power		we doubt	
I doubted		to count		we found	

▶ WORD ENDING -ther

another		brother		farther	
bother		brotherly		father	
bothered		either		feather	

gather	neither	rather
gathered	other	together
leather	others	weather
mother	otherwise	whether

▶ PHRASES

any other	I gathered	to bother
each other	many other	to gather
he gathered	other than	

▶ WORD BEGINNING *Con-*

concealed	conducted	confusion
concentrate	conductor	congested
conception	confer	congestion
concern	conference	connected
concerned	confess	connection
concerns	confine	connections
concert	confined	conscientious
concession	confirm	consent
conclude	confiscate	conservative
concluded	confiscation	consider
conclusion	conflict	considerably
conclusive	confuse	consideration
concrete	confused	considered
conduct	confusing	consign

consigned	constructive	controversy
consignee	contact	convention
consignment	contest	conversation
consist	contract	conversion
consisted	contracted	convert
consists	contractor	converted
consolidate	contracts	convey
construct	contrary	convince
constructed	contrast	reconcile
construction	control	reconstruction

▶ WORD BEGINNING *Com-*

accommodate	committee	competitive
accomplish	commodities	competitor
accomplished	commodity	competitors
combine	common	compiled
comedies	commonly	complaint
command	compact	complete
commence	comparative	completed
commend	compare	completely
comment	compared	completion
commerce	compel	compliment
commercial	compelled	complimentary
commitments	compensation	comply
committed	compete	composed

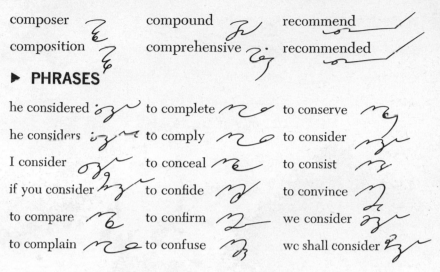

| composer | compound | recommend |
| composition | comprehensive | recommended |

▶ PHRASES

he considered	to complete	to conserve
he considers	to comply	to consider
I consider	to conceal	to consist
if you consider	to confide	to convince
to compare	to confirm	we consider
to complain	to confuse	wc shall consider

Lesson 21

▶ BRIEF FORMS

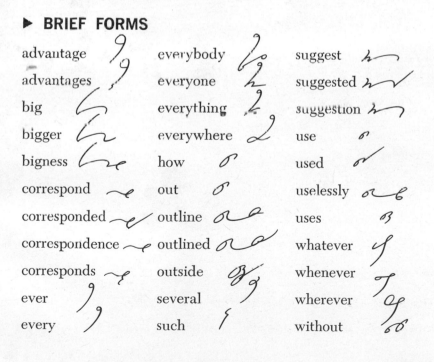

advantage	everybody	suggest
advantages	everyone	suggested
big	everything	suggestion
bigger	everywhere	use
bigness	how	used
correspond	out	uselessly
corresponded	outline	uses
correspondence	outlined	whatever
corresponds	outside	whenever
ever	several	wherever
every	such	without

▶ PHRASES

Ever, Every

ever since 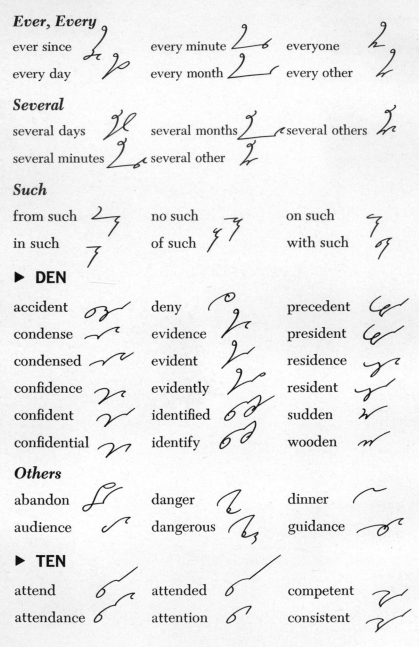	every minute	everyone
every day	every month	every other

Several

several days	several months	several others
several minutes	several other	

Such

from such	no such	on such
in such	of such	with such

▶ DEN

accident	deny	precedent
condense	evidence	president
condensed	evident	residence
confidence	evidently	resident
confident	identified	sudden
confidential	identify	wooden

Others

abandon	danger	dinner
audience	dangerous	guidance

▶ TEN

attend	attended	competent
attendance	attention	consistent

consistently   rotten   tend

content   sentence   tendency

contention   stenographer   tender

gotten   stenographic   tendered

maintenance   straighten   tent

patent   straightened   tentative

retention   tenant   written

▶ TAN

acceptance   hesitancy   stand

assistance   outstanding   standard

assistant   remittance   standing

constant   remittances   standpoint

constantly   resistance   stands

▶ TON

button   carton   tonight

▶ TIN

bulletin   contingency   itinerary

continent   contingent   satin

▶ TAIN

ascertain   certainty   curtain

attainment   contain   detained

certain   contained   fountain

certainly   container   maintain

maintained 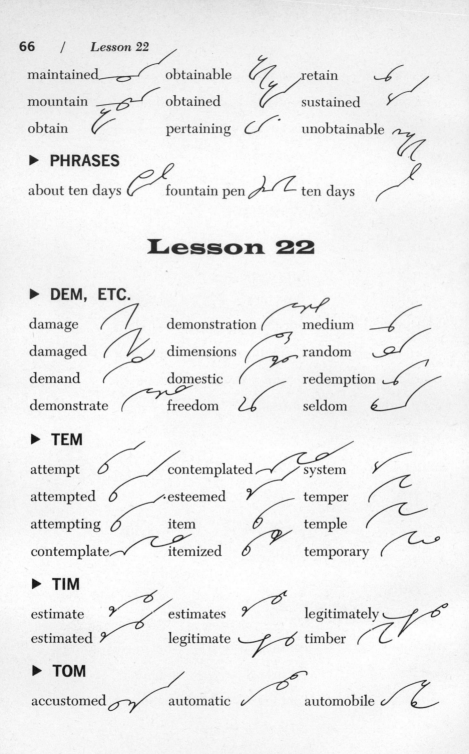 obtainable retain

mountain obtained sustained

obtain pertaining unobtainable

▶ PHRASES

about ten days fountain pen ten days

Lesson 22

▶ DEM, ETC.

damage demonstration medium

damaged dimensions random

demand domestic redemption

demonstrate freedom seldom

▶ TEM

attempt contemplated system

attempted esteemed temper

attempting item temple

contemplate itemized temporary

▶ TIM

estimate estimates legitimately

estimated legitimate timber

▶ TOM

accustomed automatic automobile

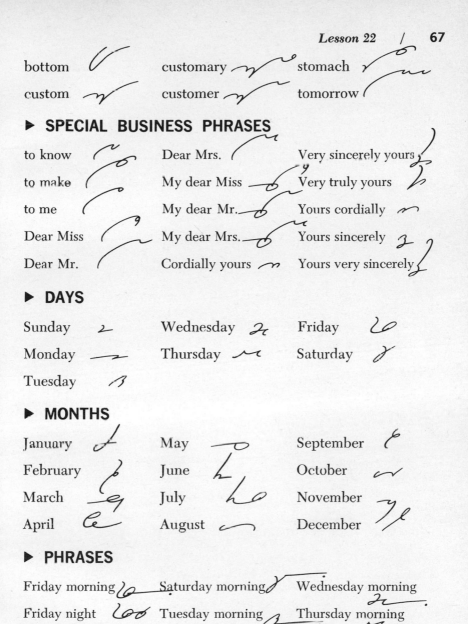

bottom   customary   stomach

custom   customer   tomorrow

▶ SPECIAL BUSINESS PHRASES

to know	Dear Mrs.	Very sincerely yours
to make	My dear Miss	Very truly yours
to me	My dear Mr.	Yours cordially
Dear Miss	My dear Mrs.	Yours sincerely
Dear Mr.	Cordially yours	Yours very sincerely

▶ DAYS

Sunday	Wednesday	Friday
Monday	Thursday	Saturday
Tuesday		

▶ MONTHS

January	May	September
February	June	October
March	July	November
April	August	December

▶ PHRASES

Friday morning	Saturday morning	Wednesday morning
Friday night	Tuesday morning	Thursday morning

Lesson 23

▶ **BRIEF FORMS**

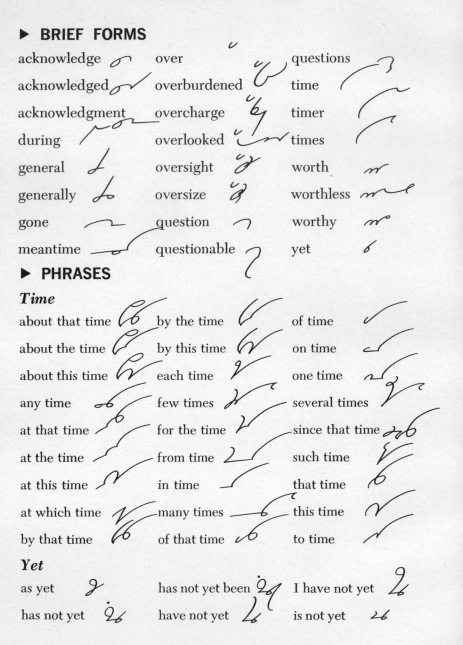

acknowledge	over	questions
acknowledged	overburdened	time
acknowledgment	overcharge	timer
during	overlooked	times
general	oversight	worth
generally	oversize	worthless
gone	question	worthy
meantime	questionable	yet

▶ **PHRASES**

Time

about that time	by the time	of time
about the time	by this time	on time
about this time	each time	one time
any time	few times	several times
at that time	for the time	since that time
at the time	from time	such time
at this time	in time	that time
at which time	many times	this time
by that time	of that time	to time

Yet

as yet	has not yet been	I have not yet
has not yet	have not yet	is not yet

Miscellaneous

has gone    have gone   in question

▶ DEF, DIF

defect		deferred		differ	
defense		definite		difference	
defer		defy		different	

▶ DIV, DEV

develop		devised		diverted	
developed		devote		divide	
development		devoted		divided	
develops		diversified		dividend	
device		diversion		division	
devise		divert		divisions	

▶ OMISSION OF *E* FROM *Ū*

absolute		continued		duly	
avenue		continues		education	
casually		continuous		educational	
communicate		due		enumerated	
communication		dues		induce	
communities		duly		inducement	
community		duplicate		issue	
continuance		duplicated		issued	
continue		duplication		issues	

knew	produce	renew
lieu	produced	renewal
manuscript	producers	renewed
monument	produces	revenue
music	pursuant	student
new	pursue	suit
newer	pursued	suitable
newest	pursuit	suited
news	reduce	visual
numerous	reduced	volume
overdue	reduces	volumes

▶ **PHRASES**

he knew	to continue	we continue
I knew	to produce	we knew
in lieu	to pursue	you knew

Chapter
5

Lesson 25

▶ **BRIEF FORMS**

difficult	requested	statement
difficulty	requests	states
envelope	satisfaction	success
envelopes	satisfactorily	under
estate	satisfactory	undercharges
next	satisfied	undersized
progress	satisfy	understand
progressive	state	understandable
request	stated	understood

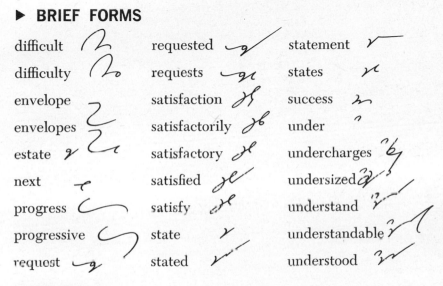

▶ **PHRASES**

Next

next meeting   next morning   next time

next month   next ten days   next year

▶ **WORDS MODIFIED IN PHRASES**

As soon as

as soon as   as soon as possible   as soon as the

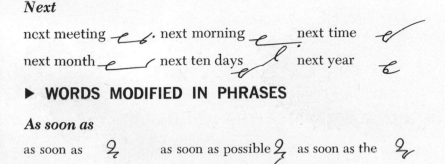

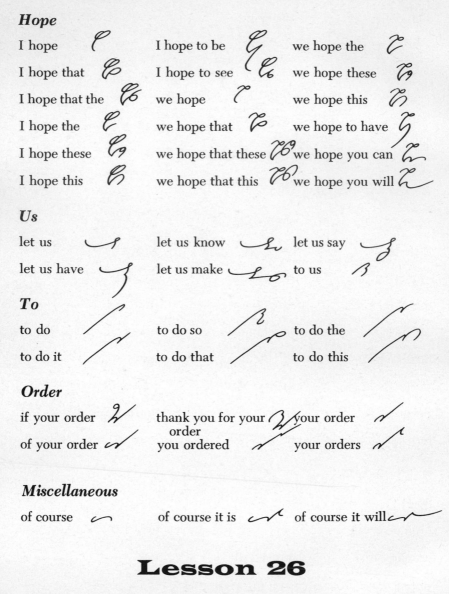

Hope

I hope

I hope that

I hope that the

I hope the

I hope these

I hope this

I hope to be

I hope to see

we hope

we hope that

we hope that these

we hope that this

we hope the

we hope these

we hope this

we hope to have

we hope you can

we hope you will

Us

let us

let us have

let us know

let us make

let us say

to us

To

to do

to do it

to do so

to do that

to do the

to do this

Order

if your order

of your order

thank you for your order

you ordered

your order

your orders

Miscellaneous

of course

of course it is

of course it will

Lesson 26

▶ **ANY VOWEL AFTER THE DIPHTHONG ī**

amplifier

appliance

bias

client	diamond	quiet
compliance	diet	science
defiance	drier	scientific
diagnosis	flier	trial
dial	prior	via
diameter	proprietor	violation

▶ THE DOTTED CIRCLE

appreciate	association	depreciation
appreciated	bacteria	initiative
appreciation	beneficiary	librarian
appreciative	brilliant	obviate
appropriate	comedian	piano
appropriation	create	radiation
area	created	radiator
areas	creative	variation

▶ WORD BEGINNING *In-*

incapable	inclined	increase
incentive	include	increased
inch	included	increases
incident	includes	incurred
incidental	inclusive	indebted
incidentally	incomprehensible	indebtedness
inclement	incorporated	indeed

indemnity

inspiration

intended

infants

install

intends

infer

installation

intention

inferior

installed

intimate

inferred

installment

intimated

influence

instance

invariably

influences

instant

inventory

injured

instead

invest

injuries

instruct

invested

injury

instructed

investigate

inlaid

instruction

investigation

insert

instructive

investment

inserted

instructor

invite

insertion

instrument

invited

inside

insurance

invoice

insist

insure

invoiced

insisted

insured

invoices

inspection

intend

involved

▶ WORD BEGINNING *Un-*

uncertain

unduly

unless

uncompromising

unfair

unloaded

uncontrollable

unfilled

unpacked

undecided

uninsured

unpaid

undoubtedly

unjust

unreasonable

unsatisfactory _⟋ℓ_   unsettled _⟋‿_   until _ℯ_

▶ **WORD BEGINNING** *Unn-*

unknown _⌐ℯ_   unnecessary _⌐ℓℓ_   unnoticed _⌐ℓ_

▶ **WORD BEGINNING** *En-*

encountered _⟋_	engagement _⟋_	enjoyed _⟋_
encourage _⟋_	engine _ℓ_	enjoyment _ℓ_
encouragement _⟋_	engineer _ℓ_	enlarge _beℓ_
encroachment _⟋_	engineers _ℓℯ_	enrolled _⌐_
endeavor _ℓℓ_	engrave _ℓℯ⟋_	en route _⌐_
engage _⟋_	engraver _⟋_	enthusiasm _ℬ_
engaged _⟋_	enjoy _ℓ_	enthusiastic _ℬℴ_

▶ **PHRASES**

we insist _⟋_   we invite _⟋_   you intend _⌐⟋_

we intend _⟋_   who intend _⟋_   your intention _⌐⟋_

Lesson 27

▶ **BRIEF FORMS**

idea _ℓ_	particulars _⟋_	speak _ℰ_
ideas _ℓ_	probable _⟋_	speaker _ℰ_
newspaper _ℶ_	probably _⟋_	speaks _ℰ_
particular _⟋_	regular _⟋_	street _ᵧ_
particularly _⟋_	regularly _⟋_	streets _ᵧ_

subject	subjected	upon

▶ **PHRASES**

in particular	upon the	upon us
to speak	upon them	upon which
upon such	upon this	upon you

▶ **NG**

along	language	song
angle	length	spring
belong	long	strength
bring	longer	string
hanger	ring	strong
hung	shingle	strongly
king	sing	swing
kingdom	single	wrong

▶ **PHRASES**

along the	along those	long time
along this	as long	so long

▶ **NGK**

anchor	banker	crank
ankle	bankruptcy	drinking
anxious	banquet	frank
anxiously	blank	frankly
bank	blanket	handkerchief

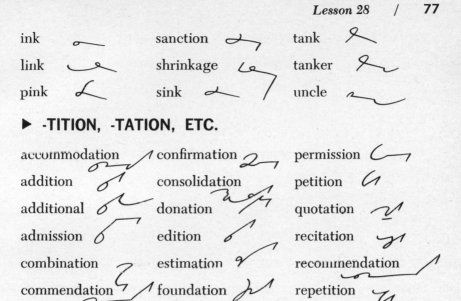

ink		sanction		tank	
link		shrinkage		tanker	
pink		sink		uncle	

▶ -TITION, -TATION, ETC.

accommodation	confirmation	permission
addition	consolidation	petition
additional	donation	quotation
admission	edition	recitation
combination	estimation	recommendation
commendation	foundation	repetition
commission	hesitation	reputation
commissioner	invitation	station
competition	notation	stationed
condition	omission	stationery

Lesson 28

▶ AH, AW

ahead		awaiting		awarded	
await		awake		aware	
awaited		award		away	

▶ Y

yacht		yard		yarn	

yarns		yellow		yoke	
yeast		yes		young	
yell		yield		youth	

► X

affix		fixes		perplexing	
appendix		flax		tax	
approximate		flexible		taxed	
box		index		taxes	
boxed		indexes		taxation	
boxes		maximum		taxicab	
fix		mix		text	
fixed		mixer		textile	

► OMISSION OF SHORT Ŭ

Before n

apron		fun		run	
begun		fund		runner	
blunder		fundamental		runs	
bunch		gallon		second	
bundles		gun		secondary	
comparison		lunch		son	
country		luncheon		sun	
done		punch		ton	
front		refund		tonnage	

Before m

become  lump   somewhere

bumper plumbing sum

column some summary

come somebody summer

drum something summons

income sometime vacuum

lumber sometimes welcome

Before a downstroke

among flush rushed

brush functions rushing

brushed judge tongue

budget judgment touch

clutch junction touched

conjunction much trunk

crushed rush trunks

▶ PHRASES

among the being done has done

among them can be done have done

among these cannot be done how much

among those can't be done I come

as much could be done I have done

be done has come must be done

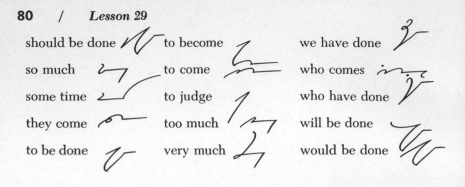

should be done · to become · we have done

so much · to come · who comes

some time · to judge · who have done

they come · too much · will be done

to be done · very much · would be done

Lesson 29

▶ BRIEF FORMS

circular · organize · publishers

circulars · public · purpose

opinion · publication · purposes

ordinarily · publications · regard

ordinary · publish · regards

organization · published · responsible

▶ PHRASES

in our opinion · in regard · to publish

▶ WORD BEGINNING *Ex-*

eccentric · examiner · exception

exact · example · exceptionally

exactly · exceed · excess

examination · exceeding · excessive

examine · excellent · excessively

examined · except · exchange

excited

expected

exposition

exclude

expects

express

exclusive

expedite

expressed

excuse

expend

expression

excuses

expended

extend

executed

expense

extended

executive

expenses

extends

exemption

expensive

extension

exhaust

experiment

extensive

exhausted

experimental

extensively

exhibit

expert

extent

exhibited

expiration

exterior

exhibition

expire

extra

exist

expired

extraordinary

existed

expires

extras

existence

explain

extreme

exists

explained

extremely

expansion

explains

inexcusable

expect

explanation

inexpensive

▶ MD, MT

ashamed

emptied

framed

claimed

empty

fumed

confirmed

exempt

gummed

deemed

famed

jammed

named   promptly   seemed

prompt   promptness   trimmed

▶ WORD ENDING -ful

awful   faithful   hopefully

beautiful   grateful   powerful

careful   gratefully   respectfully

carefully   helpful   thoughtful

delightful   helpfulness   useful

doubtful   hopeful   usefulness

Chapter 6

Lesson 31

▶ BRIEF FORMS

between	never	shortage
experience	nevertheless	shortages
experienced	quantities	shorten
experiences	quantity	shorter
inexperienced	recognize	shortest
merchandise	recognized	shortly
merchant	short	situation

▶ PHRASES

between the	between this	between us
between these	between those	between your

▶ WORD ENDING -ure

century	future	moisture
expenditure	lecture	natural
failure	literature	naturally
feature	mature	nature
fixtures	miniature	pasture

83

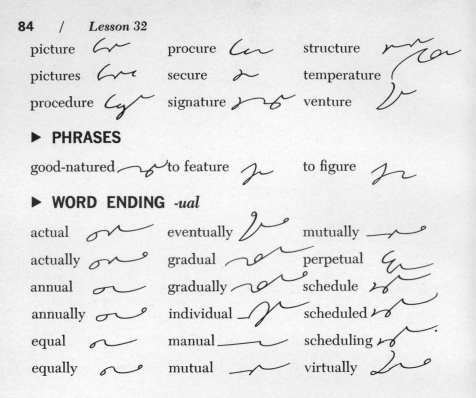

picture	procure	structure
pictures	secure	temperature
procedure	signature	venture

▶ PHRASES

good-natured   to feature   to figure

▶ WORD ENDING -*ual*

actual	eventually	mutually
actually	gradual	perpetual
annual	gradually	schedule
annually	individual	scheduled
equal	manual	scheduling
equally	mutual	virtually

Lesson 32

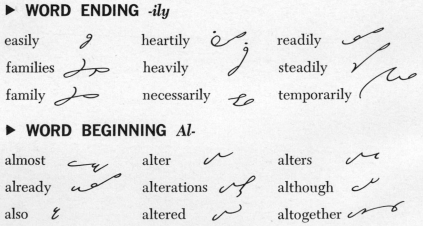

▶ WORD ENDING -*ily*

easily	heartily	readily
families	heavily	steadily
family	necessarily	temporarily

▶ WORD BEGINNING *Al-*

almost	alter	alters
already	alterations	although
also	altered	altogether

▶ **WORD BEGINNING** *Mis-*

miscarry ___ misplaced ___ misunderstanding ___

mislaid ___ mistake ___ misunderstood ___

misleading ___ mistaken ___ mystery ___

▶ **WORD BEGINNING** *Dis-*

disappoint ___ discrepancy ___ dispatch ___

disastrous ___ discretion ___ display ___

disbursed ___ discrimination ___ disposal ___

disclose ___ discuss ___ dispose ___

discontinue ___ discussed ___ disposed ___

discontinued ___ discussion ___ disposition ___

discount ___ disinclination ___ dispute ___

discounted ___ dislike ___ dissolved ___

discouraged ___ dismiss ___ distance ___

discovered ___ dismissal ___ district ___

▶ **WORD BEGINNING** *Des-*

describe ___ despite ___ destiny ___

description ___ destination ___ destroy ___

descriptive ___ destined ___ destroyed ___

▶ **PHRASES**

he discussed ___ I described ___ I discussed ___

Lesson 33

▶ **BRIEF FORMS**

character	government	railroad
characters	object	railroads
govern	objection	throughout
governed	objective	world

▶ **PHRASES**

business world   throughout the   to govern

▶ **WORD BEGINNINGS** *For-, Fore-*

afford	forerunner	forth
effort	forget	fortune
efforts	forgive	fourth
force	form	inform
forced	formal	information
foreclosure	former	informed
foreman	formerly	misfortune
foremen	forms	unfortunate

▶ **WORD BEGINNING** *Fur-*

furlough	furnish	furniture
furnace	furnished	further
furnaces	furnishing	furthermore

▶ **PHRASES**

inform us   inform you   informing us

set forth   to forego   to form

setting forth   to forfeit   to furnish

to force   to forget   to perform

▶ *Ago* **IN PHRASES**

about ten days ago   long ago   some time ago

centuries ago   months ago   some years ago

few days ago   several days ago   weeks ago

few months ago   several months ago   years ago

Lesson 34

▶ *Want* **IN PHRASES**

he wanted   if you want   who want

he wants   they want   who wanted

I want   we want   you want

I wanted   we wanted   you wanted

▶ **ORT**

assorted   headquarters   quarter

assortment   mortal   quarterly

court   port   report

deportment   portable   reported

export   ports   reports

exportation   quart   resort

sort	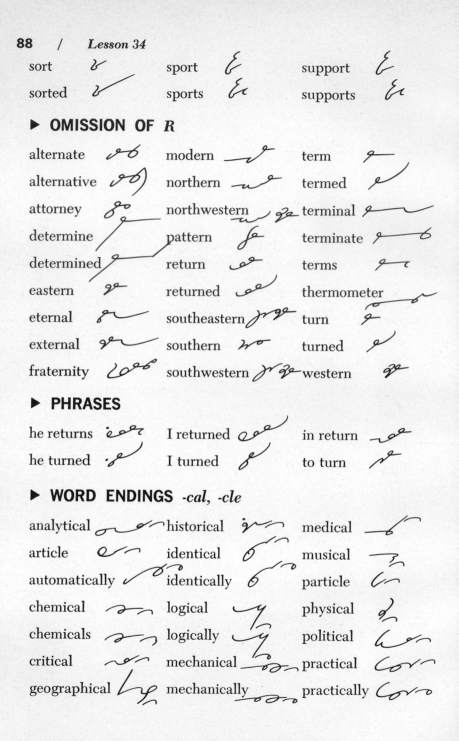	sport		support	
sorted		sports		supports	

▶ OMISSION OF *R*

alternate	modern	term
alternative	northern	termed
attorney	northwestern	terminal
determine	pattern	terminate
determined	return	terms
eastern	returned	thermometer
eternal	southeastern	turn
external	southern	turned
fraternity	southwestern	western

▶ PHRASES

he returns	I returned	in return
he turned	I turned	to turn

▶ WORD ENDINGS *-cal, -cle*

analytical	historical	medical
article	identical	musical
automatically	identically	particle
chemical	logical	physical
chemicals	logically	political
critical	mechanical	practical
geographical	mechanically	practically

radical 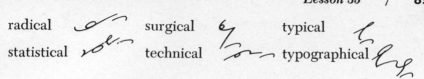   surgical   typical

statistical   technical   typographical

Lesson 35

▶ **WORD BEGINNING** *Inter-*

interest	interim	interpreted
interested	interior	interrupted
interesting	intermediate	interruption
interests	internal	interval
interfere	international	interview
interference	interpretation	

▶ **WORD BEGINNING** *Intr-*

introduce   introduced   introduction

▶ **WORD BEGINNINGS** *Enter-, Entr-*

enter	enterprise	entrance
entered	entertain	entrances
entering	entertainment	unenterprising

▶ **WORD ENDING** *-ings*

bearings	clippings	feelings
beginnings	drawings	furnishings
buildings	earnings	hearings
casings	evenings	holdings

linings	openings	proceedings
meetings	paintings	savings
offerings	pleadings	servings

▶ PHRASES

Friday mornings	so many things
in this morning's	such things
many things	this morning's

▶ WORDS OMITTED IN PHRASES

at a loss	glad to see
at a time	I am of the opinion
at such a time	in a few days
bill of sale	in a few months
by the way	in a position
during the last	in addition to the
during the past	in addition to this
for a few days	in order to be
for a few minutes	in order to become
for a long time	in relation to the
for a minute	in such a manner
for a moment	in the future
glad to have	in the past
glad to know	in the world
glad to say	line of business

line of goods		out of the	
many of the		out of the question	
many of them		out of them	
men and women		out of this	
none of the		some of our	
none of them		some of the	
on the subject		some of them	
one of our		some of these	
one of the		some of this	
one of the best		some of those	
one of the most		son-in-law	
one of them		such a thing	
one of these		two or three	
one of those		up and down	
one or two		up to date	
ought to have		we are of the opinion	
out of date		week or two	
out of that		will you please	

Chapter 7

Lesson 37

▶ **WORD ENDING** *-ingly*

accordingly 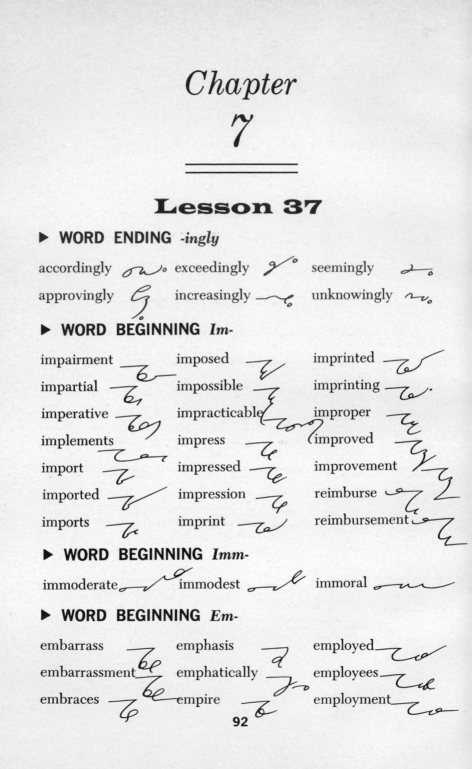 exceedingly   seemingly

approvingly   increasingly   unknowingly

▶ **WORD BEGINNING** *Im-*

impairment	imposed	imprinted
impartial	impossible	imprinting
imperative	impracticable	improper
implements	impress	improved
import	impressed	improvement
imported	impression	reimburse
imports	imprint	reimbursement

▶ **WORD BEGINNING** *Imm-*

immoderate   immodest   immoral

▶ **WORD BEGINNING** *Em-*

embarrass	emphasis	employed
embarrassment	emphatically	employees
embraces	empire	employment

► **OMISSION OF MINOR VOWEL**

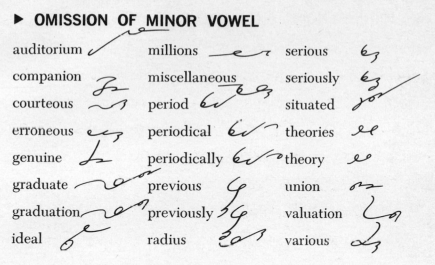

auditorium	millions	serious
companion	miscellaneous	seriously
courteous	period	situated
erroneous	periodical	theories
genuine	periodically	theory
graduate	previous	union
graduation	previously	valuation
ideal	radius	various

Lesson 38

► **WORD ENDING** *-ship*

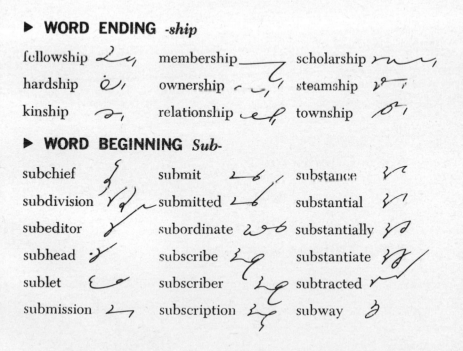

fellowship	membership	scholarship
hardship	ownership	steamship
kinship	relationship	township

► **WORD BEGINNING** *Sub-*

subchief	submit	substance
subdivision	submitted	substantial
subeditor	subordinate	substantially
subhead	subscribe	substantiate
sublet	subscriber	subtracted
submission	subscription	subway

▶ JOINING HOOK AND CIRCLE VOWELS

drawee	poets	radios
poems	portfolio	rayon
poetry	radio	snowy

Lesson 39

▶ WORD ENDING -rity

authorities	majority	securities
charity	maturity	security
clarity	prosperity	surety

▶ WORD ENDING -lity

ability	inability	possibilities
advisability	liabilities	qualities
disability	locality	reliability
facilities	nobility	responsibility
facility	personality	sensibilities

▶ WORD ENDING -lty

casualty	loyalty	royalties
faculty	penalty	royalty

▶ WORD ENDINGS -self, -selves

herself	itself	oneself
himself	myself	ourselves

| themselves ⌒꜌ | yourself ꜋ | yourselves ꜋ |

► **PHRASES**

for itself ꜀	for themselves ↗	in itself ⌐
for myself ⌐	for yourself ꜋	of ourselves ⌐
for ourselves ⌐	for yourselves ꜋	with themselves ⌐

Lesson 40

► **ABBREVIATING PRINCIPLE**

-tribute, -tribution

attribute	contribution	distribution
contribute	distribute	distributors
contributed	distributed	retribution

-quent

| consequently | eloquent | frequently |
| delinquent | frequent | subsequent |

-quire

acquire	inquire	require
acquirement	inquiries	required
esquire	inquiry	requirements

-titute, -titution

| constitute | institution | substitute |
| institute | restitution | substitution |

-titude

aptitude 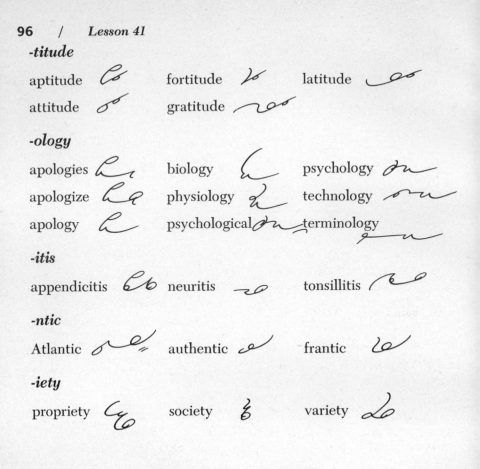   fortitude   latitude

attitude   gratitude

-ology

apologies   biology   psychology

apologize   physiology   technology

apology   psychological   terminology

-itis

appendicitis   neuritis   tonsillitis

-ntic

Atlantic   authentic   frantic

-iety

propriety   society   variety

Lesson 41

▶ **ABBREVIATING PRINCIPLE** (*Concluded*)

algebra   convenient   inconvenienced

alphabet   conveniently   inconvenient

alphabetical   curriculum   memoranda

arithmetic   equivalent   memorandum

convenience   inconvenience   memorandums

philosophy 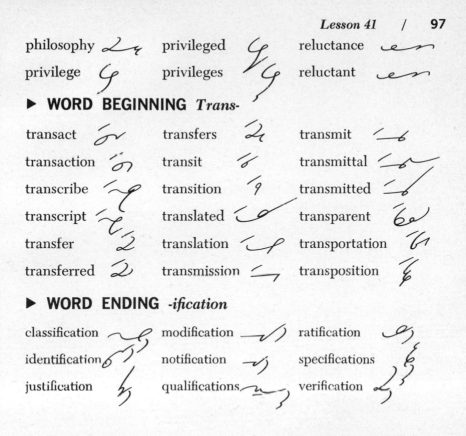   privileged   reluctance

privilege   privileges   reluctant

▶ **WORD BEGINNING** *Trans-*

transact   transfers   transmit

transaction   transit   transmittal

transcribe   transition   transmitted

transcript   translated   transparent

transfer   translation   transportation

transferred   transmission   transposition

▶ **WORD ENDING** *-ification*

classification   modification   ratification

identification   notification   specifications

justification   qualifications   verification

Chapter

8

Lesson 43

▶ **WORD ENDING** *-ulate*

accumulate 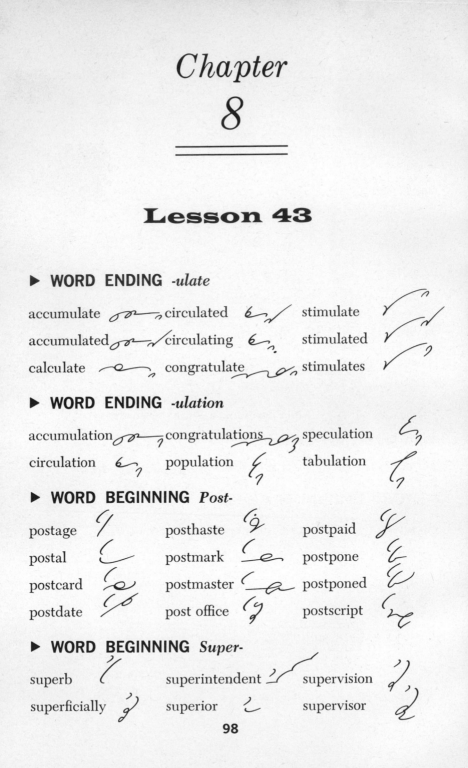 circulated   stimulate

accumulated   circulating   stimulated

calculate   congratulate   stimulates

▶ **WORD ENDING** *-ulation*

accumulation   congratulations   speculation

circulation   population   tabulation

▶ **WORD BEGINNING** *Post-*

postage   posthaste   postpaid

postal   postmark   postpone

postcard   postmaster   postponed

postdate   post office   postscript

▶ **WORD BEGINNING** *Super-*

superb   superintendent   supervision

superficially   superior   supervisor

Lesson 44

▶ **WORD ENDING** *-sume*

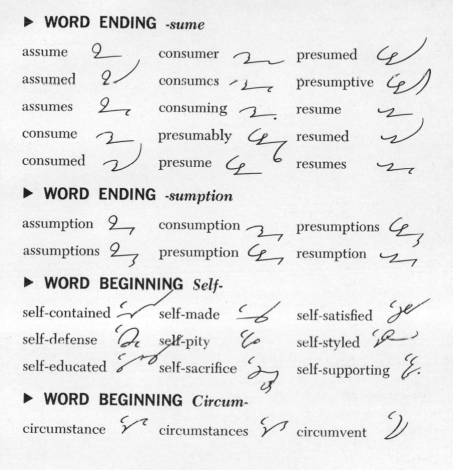

assume	consumer	presumed
assumed	consumes	presumptive
assumes	consuming	resume
consume	presumably	resumed
consumed	presume	resumes

▶ **WORD ENDING** *-sumption*

assumption	consumption	presumptions
assumptions	presumption	resumption

▶ **WORD BEGINNING** *Self-*

self-contained	self-made	self-satisfied
self-defense	self-pity	self-styled
self-educated	self-sacrifice	self-supporting

▶ **WORD BEGINNING** *Circum-*

circumstance	circumstances	circumvent

Lesson 45

▶ **WORD ENDING** *-hood*

boyhood	hardihood	neighborhood
childhood	manhood	parenthood

▶ **WORD ENDING** *-ward*

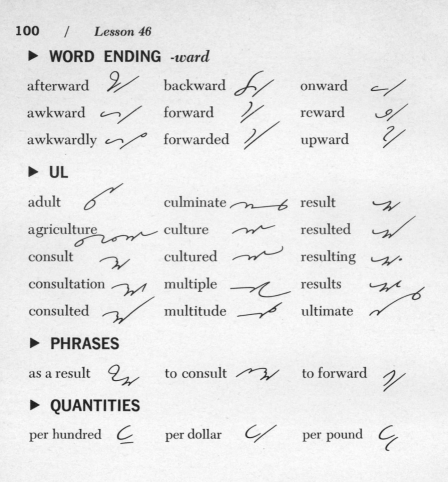

afterward	backward	onward
awkward	forward	reward
awkwardly	forwarded	upward

▶ **UL**

adult	culminate	result
agriculture	culture	resulted
consult	cultured	resulting
consultation	multiple	results
consulted	multitude	ultimate

▶ **PHRASES**

as a result	to consult	to forward

▶ **QUANTITIES**

per hundred	per dollar	per pound

Lesson 46

▶ **WORD ENDING** *-gram*

cablegram	monogram	telegram
diagram	program	telegrams

▶ **WORD BEGINNINGS** *Electric, Electr-*

electric	electrical	electrically

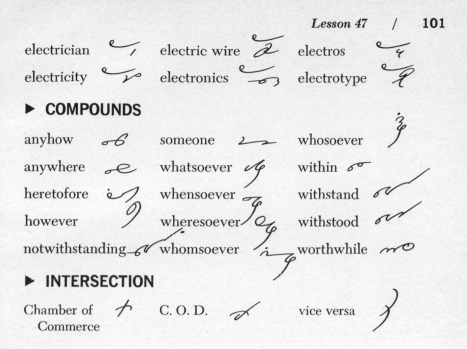

electrician   electric wire   electros

electricity   electronics   electrotype

▶ COMPOUNDS

anyhow   someone   whosoever

anywhere   whatsoever   within

heretofore   whensoever   withstand

however   wheresoever   withstood

notwithstanding   whomsoever   worthwhile

▶ INTERSECTION

Chamber of   C. O. D.   vice versa
Commerce

Lesson 47

▶ GEOGRAPHICAL TERMINATIONS

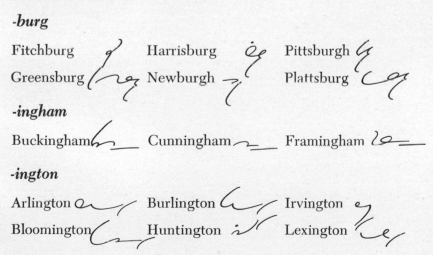

-burg

Fitchburg   Harrisburg   Pittsburgh

Greensburg   Newburgh   Plattsburg

-ingham

Buckingham   Cunningham   Framingham

-ington

Arlington   Burlington   Irvington

Bloomington   Huntington   Lexington

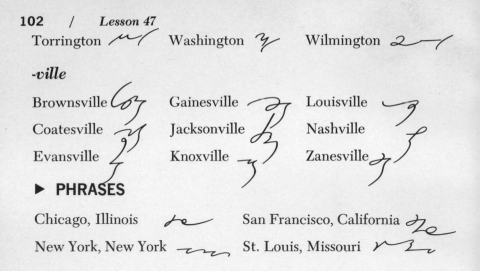

Torrington ⟋⟍⟋ Washington ⟋⟋ Wilmington ⟋⟋⟋

-ville

Brownsville ⟋⟋ Gainesville ⟋⟋ Louisville ⟋⟋

Coatesville ⟋⟋ Jacksonville ⟋⟋ Nashville ⟋⟋

Evansville ⟋⟋ Knoxville ⟋⟋ Zanesville ⟋⟋

▶ **PHRASES**

Chicago, Illinois ⟋⟋ San Francisco, California ⟋⟋

New York, New York ⟋⟋ St. Louis, Missouri ⟋⟋

Appendix

The 500 most-used words presented in the order of their frequency in the Horn-Peterson "The Vocabulary of Business Letters."

1. I	17. be	33. my
2. the	18. are	34. had
3. and	19. not	35. our
4. to	20. as	36. from
5. a	21. order	37. am
6. you	22. at	38. one
7. of	23. this	39. time
8. in	24. with	40. he
9. we	25. but	41. received
10. for	26. on	42. get
11. it	27. if	43. please
12. that	28. all	44. do
13. is	29. so	45. been
14. your	30. me	46. letter
15. have	31. was	47. can
16. will	32. very	48. would

103

49. she
50. when
51. about
52. they
53. any
54. which
55. some
56. has
57. attention
58. matter
59. or
60. there
61. send
62. kindly
63. us
64. good
65. account
66. know
67. just
68. make
69. by
70. up
71. day
72. much

73. copy
74. made
75. same
76. out
77. her
78. also
79. yours
80. now
81. well
82. an
83. here
84. find
85. sent
86. them
87. glad
88. shipment
89. return
90. see
91. information
92. price
93. check
94. give
95. amount
96. advise

97. go
98. receipt
99. what
100. enclosed
101. note
102. come
103. were
104. credit
105. no
106. thank
107. how
108. herewith
109. however
110. other
111. wish
112. did
113. say
114. him
115. take
116. date
117. possible
118. his
119. got
120. work

121. over
122. number
123. may
124. company
125. present
126. before
127. hope
128. business
129. sending
130. only
131. being
132. two
133. balance
134. after
135. appreciate
136. regarding
137. service
138. more
139. first
140. could
141. enclosing
142. reply
143. interest
144. shall

145. receive
146. today
147. too
148. office
149. must
150. satisfactory
151. should
152. returned
153. like
154. year
155. their
156. covering
157. pleased
158. favor
159. stock
160. thanking
161. who
162. necessary
163. believe
164. department
165. line
166. therefore
167. cannot
168. forward

169. making
170. new
171. payment
172. sir
173. future
174. material
175. book
176. days
177. able
178. best
179. let
180. cover
181. trust
182. state
183. prices
184. feel
185. soon
186. further
187. next
188. through
189. above
190. bill
191. case
192. last

193. again
194. statement
195. care
196. think
197. each
198. upon
199. thing
200. list
201. want
202. given
203. way
204. part
205. kind
206. regard
207. returning
208. reference
209. hand
210. call
211. request
212. these
213. such
214. special
215. remittance
216. mail

217. three
218. fact
219. use
220. write
221. course
222. goods
223. size
224. hear
225. few
226. pleasure
227. desire
228. right
229. following
230. unable
231. past
232. referring
233. shipped
234. until
235. every
236. without
237. prompt
238. taken
239. month
240. week

241. old
242. cost
243. report
244. charge
245. writing
246. paid
247. orders
248. little
249. invoice
250. furnish
251. remain
252. might
253. once
254. yet
255. another
256. put
257. interested
258. replying
259. since
260. expect
261. records
262. man
263. place
264. back

265. promptly
266. delay
267. understand
268. money
269. sorry
270. bank
271. opportunity
272. than
273. ordered
274. whether
275. complete
276. attached
277. recent
278. regret
279. used
280. sure
281. school
282. car
283. connection
284. sales
285. enclose
286. going
287. books
288. because

289. better
290. giving
291. supply
292. contract
293. general
294. its
295. within
296. city
297. small
298. accept
299. having
300. during
301. many
302. position
303. subject
304. direct
305. always
306. sale
307. ago
308. need
309. full
310. reason
311. ask
312. off

313. under
314. several
315. big
316. both
317. value
318. acknowledge
319. own
320. change
321. file
322. offer
323. item
324. pay
325. freight
326. advance
327. name
328. try
329. advised
330. dated
331. boy
332. forwarded
333. items
334. bad
335. placed
336. separate

337. against
338. anything
339. great
340. greatly
341. written
342. claim
343. entirely
344. high
345. look
346. short
347. instructions
348. requested
349. additional
350. early
351. done
352. still
353. convenience
354. doubt
355. called
356. open
357. show
358. express
359. wrote
360. correct

361. condition
362. notice
363. years
364. merchandise
365. copies
366. long
367. original
368. large
369. bring
370. sample
371. catalogue
372. enough
373. careful
374. while
375. wire
376. already
377. ship
378. people
379. into
380. either
381. most
382. does
383. suggest
384. delivery

385. keep
386. second
387. assure
388. immediate
389. later
390. probably
391. bed
392. found
393. getting
394. duplicate
395. lot
396. seems
397. rate
398. consider
399. paper
400. refer
401. error
402. discount
403. shipping
404. indeed
405. collection
406. less
407. together
408. customer

409. gentlemen
410. consideration
411. inquiry
412. address
413. answer
414. asked
415. recently
416. appreciated
417. men
418. question
419. form
420. purchase
421. doing
422. charged
423. trusting
424. certainly
425. oblige
426. proper
427. writer
428. asking
429. sell
430. taking
431. total
432. why

433. record
434. showing
435. help
436. nothing
437. action
438. charges
439. settlement
440. expense
441. accordance
442. along
443. near
444. policy
445. unless
446. mind
447. correspondence
448. quite
449. rather
450. card
451. factory
452. far
453. calling
454. meet
455. weeks
456. sold

457. matters
458. reach
459. letters
460. particular
461. approval
462. meeting
463. stated
464. truly
465. dozen
466. close
467. saw
468. referred
469. class
470. page
471. although
472. months
473. relative
474. memorandum
475. addressed
476. arrange
477. handle
478. between
479. regular
480. cash

481. personal
488. morning
495. handling

482. trouble
489. house
496. secure

483. coming
490. draft
497. something

484. point
491. advertising
498. basis

485. different
492. earliest
499. wishes

486. entire
493. hold
500. certain

487. issue
494. cases

Index to Words

(Note: *a, 3* means that the word may first be written in Lesson 3, in *Gregg Shorthand, Diamond Jubilee Series.*)

A

a, 3
abandon, 21
ability, 39
able, 3
abnormal, 5
about, 15
above, 13
abroad, 7
absence, 5
absent, 10
absolute, 23
absorb, 5
accept, 5
acceptable, 15
acceptance, 21
accepted, 14
access, 10
accident, 21
accommodate, 20
accommodation, 27
accompanied, 19
accomplish, 20
accomplished, 20
accordance, 11
accordingly, 37
account, 20
accountant, 20
accounted, 20
accrued, 5
accumulate, 43
accumulated, 43
accumulation, 43
accurate, 5
accusation, 19
accuse, 19
accustomed, 22
acknowledge, 23
acknowledged, 23
acknowledgement, 23
acquainted, 14
acquire, 40
acquirement, 40
acre, 4
act, 5
acted, 14
action, 9
active, 5
actively, 8
activity, 5
acts, 5
actual, 31
actually, 31
acute, 19
adaptable, 15
adapted, 14
add, 5
added, 14
adding, 5
addition, 27
additional, 27
address, 5
addresses, 10
adequate, 14
adhere, 5

adjust, 13
adjustable, 15
adjusted, 14
adjustment, 19
adjusts, 13
administer, 16
admission, 27
admit, 5
admitted, 14
adopt, 7
adopted, 14
adult, 45
advance, 5
advances, 10
advantage, 21
advantages, 21
advertise, 19
advertisement, 19
advice, 5
advices, 10
advisable, 15
advisability, 39
advocate, 5
affect, 5
affected, 15
affects, 5
affix, 28
afford, 33
after, 19
aftermath, 19
afternoon, 19
afterthought, 19
afterward, 45
again, 5
against, 5
age, 4
agencies, 4
agency, 4
agent, 10
agents, 10
aggregate, 5
aging, 4
ago, 5
agree, 5
agreeable, 15
agreement, 19
agriculture, 45
ahead, 28
aid, 1
aim, 1
aiming, 2
alarm, 5
algebra, 41
all, 7
allocation, 9
allotment, 19
allow, 20
allowance, 20
allowed, 20
almost, 32
alone, 5
along, 27
aloud, 20
alphabet, 41
alphabetical, 41
already, 32

also, 32
alter, 32
alterations, 32
alternate, 34
alternative, 34
alters, 32
although, 32
altogether, 32
aluminum, 16
always, 14
am, 3
ambitious, 13
amend, 16
amended, 16
amendment, 19
among, 28
amount, 20
amounted, 20
amounts, 20
ample, 5
amplifier, 26
amplify, 5
amply, 8
an, 3
analysis, 10
analytical, 34
anchor, 27
ancient, 9
and, 11
angle, 27
ankle, 27
announce, 20
announced, 20
announcement, 20
announces, 20
annoyance, 16
annoyed, 16
annual, 31
annually, 31
annum, 13
another, 20
answer, 5
answered, 11
anticipate, 10
anticipated, 14
anticipation, 10
antique, 10
anxious, 27
anxiously, 27
any, 5
anybody, 7
anyhow, 46
anyone, 15
anything, 15
anywhere, 46
apiece, 5
apologies, 40
apologize, 40
apology, 40
apparatus, 13
apparent, 10
appeal, 5
appear, 5
appeared, 11
appendicitis, 40
appendix, 28

appliance, 20
applicable, 15
applicant, 10
application, 9
applies, 5
apply, 5
appointed, 16
appointment, 19
appreciable, 15
appreciate, 26
appreciated, 26
appreciation, 26
appreciative, 26
approach, 5
approached, 5
appropriate, 26
appropriation, 26
approval, 5
approve, 5
approved, 5
approvingly, 37
approximate, 28
April, 22
apron, 28
aptitude, 40
are, 3
area, 26
areas, 26
argue, 19
arisen, 5
arises, 10
arithmetic, 41
Arlington, 47
arm, 5
arms, 5
army, 5
around, 20
arrange, 5
arrangement, 19
arrive, 5
arrives, 5
art, 5
article, 34
artist, 5
as, 5
ascertain, 21
ashamed, 29
aside, 5
ask, 5
asserted, 14
assessed, 10
assessment, 19
assets, 5
assigned, 10
assignment, 19
assist, 10
assistance, 21
assistant, 21
association, 26
assorted, 34
assortment, 34
assume, 44
assumed, 44
assumes, 44
assumption, 44
assumptions, 44